WORLD'S BIGGEST

HEART-STOPPING Roller Coasters

by Meish Goldish

Consultant: Eric Gieszl
Editor and Founder of ultimaterollercoaster.com

BEARPORT
PUBLISHING

New York, New York

Credits

Cover and Title Page, © Chad Slattery/Stone/Getty Images and Robin Smith/Stone/Getty Images; TOC, © Chris Fourie/Shutterstock; 4, Courtesy of The Library of Congress; 5, © Chip East/Reuters/Landov; 6, © Stan Honda/AFP/Getty Images; 7, © Splash News and Pictures/Newscom; 8, © Jeff Rogers/Coaster Gallery; 9, © Fabiano Kai; 10, © Coasterimage.com; 11, © TopFoto/UPPA/Photoshot; 12, Courtesy of Cedar Point; 13, © Coasterimage.com; 14, © AP Images; 15L, © Chris Caravello/Ultimate Rollercoaster; 15R, © Eric Gieszl/Ultimate Rollercoaster; 16, © Joel Rogers/Coaster Gallery; 17, © Johnny Heger; 18, © Trevor Smith/Alamy; 19L, © Joel Rogers/Coaster Gallery; 19R, © Joel Rogers/Coaster Gallery; 20, © Jeff Rogers/Coaster Gallery; 21, Courtesy of Six Flags Great America; 22TL, © Zuma Press/Newscom; 22TR, © Benjamin Roach; 22BL, Courtesy of Beach Park; 22BR, © China Photos/Getty Images; 23TL, © Russell M. Van Tassell; 23TR, Courtesy of Six Flags Great America; 23BL, © Saga Photography/iStockphoto; 23BR, © Flashon Studio/Shutterstock.

Publisher: Kenn Goin
Editorial Director: Adam Siegel
Creative Director: Spencer Brinker
Photo Researcher: James O'Connor
Design: Debrah Kaiser

Library of Congress Cataloging-in-Publication Data

Goldish, Meish.
  Heart-stopping roller coasters / by Meish Goldish.
      p. cm. — (World's biggest)
  Includes bibliographical references and index.
  ISBN-13: 978-1-59716-956-1 (library binding)
  ISBN-10: 1-59716-956-0 (library binding)
  1. Roller coasters—Juvenile literature. I. Title.

  GV1860.R64G65 2010
  791.06'8—dc22
                                2009003067

For more information, write to Bearport Publishing Company, Inc., 101 Fifth Avenue, Suite 6R, New York, New York 10003. Printed in the United States of America.

10 9 8 7 6 5 4 3 2 1

CONTENTS

THE FIRST COASTERS IN AMERICA

	The Gravity Pleasure Switchback Railway	The Cyclone
Opened:	1884	1927
Height:	50 feet (15 m)	85 feet (26 m)
Length:	600 feet (183 m)	2,640 feet (805 m)
Speed:	6 miles per hour (9.7 kph)	60 miles per hour (97 kph)
Location:	Coney Island Amusement Park in Brooklyn, New York	

Want to take a ride you'll never forget? Then hop aboard a roller coaster. These giant "scream machines" are some of the biggest, fastest—and scariest—rides around.

The first coaster in America opened in 1884 at Coney Island Amusement Park in Brooklyn, New York. The ride was called the Gravity Pleasure Switchback Railway. It wasn't nearly as big—or as fast—as today's coasters. It had one car that moved at only six miles per hour (9.7 kph). Many adults can run faster than that!

The Gravity Pleasure Switchback Railway

Over the years, roller coasters got bigger and faster. By 1927 Coney Island had a new coaster called the Cyclone. It was about four times longer than the park's first coaster and ten times as fast. Yet today, roller coasters are even bigger, faster, and scarier!

Coney Island's Cyclone

The idea for roller coasters came from ice slides that were popular in Russia in the 1400s. People sat on a small sled and rode down a long, icy ramp for fun.

KINGDA KA

Location: Six Flags Great Adventure in Jackson, New Jersey

Opened: 2005

Height: 456 feet (139 m)

Length: 3,118 feet (950 m)

Speed: 128 miles per hour (206 kph)

All roller coasters are tall. Kingda Ka, however, is the tallest roller coaster in the world. A train of five cars blasts up a long steel track. It takes riders to the top of a tower that is 456 feet (139 m) high—as tall as a 45-story building! Then the train zooms back down. The riders scream as they fly through the air. Luckily, this heart-stopping ride lasts less than a minute.

The cars on Kingda Ka rocket from 0 to 128 miles per hour (206 kph) in just 3.5 seconds.

STEEL DRAGON
2000

Location: Nagashima Spa Land in Mie, Japan

Opened: 2000

Height: 318 feet (97 m)

Length: 8,133 feet (2,479 m)

Speed: 95 miles per hour (153 kph)

Kingda Ka is the king of height. Yet the longest roller coaster in the world is Steel Dragon 2000. Its **circuit** is made up of 8,133 feet (2,479 m) of track. That's longer than 27 football fields placed end to end! When you're zooming along at 95 miles per hour (153 kph), however, it takes only about four minutes to cover that distance.

Steel Dragon 2000 cost more than $50 million to build—and it was made to last. This huge coaster can withstand the earthquakes that sometimes shake the ground in Japan.

Steel Dragon 2000 got its name because it is made of steel and opened in 2000, the Asian Year of the Dragon.

THE BEAST

Location: Kings Island in Mason, Ohio

Opened: 1979

Height: 110 feet (34 m)

Length: 7,359 feet (2,243 m)

Speed: 64 miles per hour (103 kph)

Before people began using steel to build roller-coaster tracks, they used wood. The longest wooden coaster in the world is The Beast. Its track winds and loops for more than one mile (1.6 km). Along the way, riders blast through three dark tunnels.

Today, The Beast has a "child." Son of Beast opened in 2000. At 218 feet (66 m) high, it's the tallest wooden coaster on Earth!

Son of Beast

The Beast zooms through 35 woody acres (14 hectares) during its four minute ride.

MILLENNIUM FORCE

Location: Cedar Point Amusement Park in Sandusky, Ohio

Opened: 2000

Height: 310 feet (94 m)

Length: 6,595 feet (2,010 m)

Speed: 92 miles per hour (148 kph)

Records are made to be broken. That's what Millennium Force did. This steel coaster set ten world records when it opened, including the fastest and tallest coaster in the world!

Millennium Force's records have since been broken. Yet riders still love zooming up and down the giant coaster's hills. In fact, Millennium Force has been voted the best steel roller-coaster ride in America five times since 2001.

The ride on Millennium Force lasts about 2 minutes and 20 seconds from end to end.

SUPERMAN: THE ESCAPE

Location: Six Flags Magic Mountain in Valencia, California

Opened: 1997

Height: 415 feet (126 m)

Length: 1,315 feet (401 m)

Speed: 100 miles per hour (161 kph)

Superman: The Escape may not be faster than a speeding bullet, but it does give riders a thrill that few coasters can match. This heart-stopping ride is a **shuttle coaster**, so it doesn't just zoom along in one direction. It takes riders forward *and* backward!

After reaching a speed of 100 miles per hour (161 kph) in just seven seconds, the train blasts straight up a steel track. At the top the riders reach a height of about 400 feet (122 m). That's taller than many skyscrapers in downtown Los Angeles. Then the train drops back down to Earth—backward. The coaster flies through the air so quickly that it reaches the ground in just a few seconds.

Superman: The Escape
is the tallest shuttle
coaster in the world.

AMERICAN EAGLE

Location: Six Flags Great
America in Gurnee, Illinois

Opened: 1981

Height: 127 feet (39 m)

Length: 4,650 feet (1,417 m)

Speed: 66 miles per hour (106 kph)

Roller coasters aren't just for riding. Some are for racing. A **racing coaster** has two tracks with a train on each one. The trains race each other during the trip. Riders don't control how fast the coasters move, however. The speed depends a lot on the riders' weight and where it is placed in the cars. Races are close but almost never end in a tie.

American Eagle is the longest and fastest racing wooden roller coaster in the world. The trains travel over hills and speed through twisting tracks. During part of the race, one train even passes over the other. No wonder some riders on this coaster feel as if they're soaring like an eagle.

The American Eagle trains race each other for about 2 minutes and 35 seconds.

THE RIDDLER'S REVENGE

Location: Six Flags Magic Mountain in Valencia, California

Opened: 1998

Height: 156 feet (48 m)

Length: 4,370 feet (1,332 m)

Speed: 65 miles per hour (105 kph)

On most roller coasters, the riders sit. The Riddler's Revenge is different. Its riders stand! The Riddler's Revenge is the tallest and fastest stand-up roller coaster in the world. During the trip, riders go around many large loops. They turn upside down six times. It's a dizzying trip, but riders love it. They stand and cheer for this twisting stand-up coaster!

The Riddler's Revenge is named for the Riddler, a comic-book character who is an enemy of Batman. The ride's train and track are green, just like the Riddler's clothes.

TATSU

Location: Six Flags Magic Mountain in Valencia, California

Opened: 2006

Height: 170 feet (52 m)

Length: 3,602 feet (1,098 m)

Speed: 62 miles per hour (100 kph)

For some coaster lovers, standing isn't enough. They want to fly! Tatsu is a dream come true for them. It's the tallest, longest, and fastest **flying coaster** on Earth. Riders are fastened into their seats. Then they are turned facedown under the track. From high above, the riders look down over the park as they dive, swoop, and soar—almost as if they are flying!

Each year brings bigger and scarier roller coasters. What will builders think of next? No one knows. Yet for those who can't wait to find out, they can hop into one of the many giant scream machines rocketing through the sky today—if they are brave enough!

Six Flags Magic Mountain in Valencia, California, has 16 roller coasters. However, the record for the most roller coasters is held by Cedar Point Amusement Park in Sandusky, Ohio. It has 17!

MORE BIG RIDES

Roller coasters aren't the only big rides people enjoy.
Here are four others.

The Beijing (BAY-JING) Great Wheel
in China is the tallest Ferris wheel in
the world. It rises 682 feet (208 m)
into the air.

The world's tallest free-fall ride is the
Giant Drop in Australia. Riders sit on
a platform and drop 390 feet (119 m),
speeding 84 miles per hour (135 kph).

The tallest waterslide in the world
is the Insano in Brazil. It is 135 feet
(41 m) high. Riders slide down at 65
miles per hour (105 kph)—as fast as
most cars go on a highway.

The world's tallest bungee jump is
the Macau Tower in China. Jumpers
drop about 650 feet (198 m) in just
five seconds. They fall 124 miles
per hour (200 kph)—a speed that
is almost twice as fast as cars are
allowed to travel on a highway!

GLOSSARY

circuit (SUR-kit) a complete roller coaster track from beginning to end

flying coaster (FLYE-ing KOHSS-tur) a roller coaster where riders travel facedown under the track

racing coaster (RAY-sing KOHSS-tur) a roller coaster with two tracks so that trains can race each other

shuttle coaster (SHUHT-uhl KOHSS-tur) a roller coaster where the beginning and end of the track do not meet to make a complete circuit; instead, the train travels both forward and backward to make a complete trip

INDEX

BIBLIOGRAPHY

www.coasterglobe.com/

www.coastergrotto.com/

www.ultimaterollercoaster.com/

READ MORE

Burgan, Michael. *The World's Wildest Roller Coasters.* Mankato, MN: Capstone (2001).

Lepora, Nathan. *Marvelous Machinery: Rides at Work.* Pleasantville, NY: Gareth Stevens (2008).

Mason, Paul. *Roller Coaster!* Chicago: Raintree (2007).

Mitchell, Susan K. *The Biggest Thrill Rides.* Pleasantville, NY: Gareth Stevens (2008).

LEARN MORE ONLINE

To learn more about the biggest roller coasters, visit
www.bearportpublishing.com/WorldsBiggest

ABOUT THE AUTHOR

Meish Goldish has written more than 200 books for children. His home in Brooklyn, New York, is not far from the Cyclone at Coney Island.